Old PARKHEAD

by
Charles McDonald

This crowded picture of Edmiston Street was probably taken prior to King George V and Queen Mary's royal visit to Parkhead in July 1914. A full military dress rehearsal was held along the route from Parkhead Railway Station to Parkhead Forge, and along with the visit itself attracted large crowds.

First Published in the United Kingdom, 1996
By Stenlake Publishing
Telephone/Fax: 01290 551122

ISBN 1 872074 85 5

Miss McFarlane's Primary 1 class, London Road Primary School, 1960.

Foreword

Despite the vital role that she has played in Glasgow's development, the story of Parkhead has been given little credit in most histories of the city. The only record of life in the area that I have been able to find is the memoirs of Baillie David Willox, who was born and raised in the village – and these were written in 1920.

In 1800 the three hamlets of Camlachie, Parkhead and Westmuir consisted of mining and weaving communities. However, by 1918 Parkhead had become the largest industrial centre in Scotland, mainly due to the establishment of Sir William Beardmore's Parkhead Forge Works and other industries in the district.

At the end of the nineteenth century Britain boasted an Empire on which the sun never set, although as one Parkhead wit wrote at the time, this was possibly only because 'God would not trust an Englishman in the dark'! If Glasgow was the second city of the Empire, then Parkhead, with its heavy industry, could rightfully lay claim to being one of the engine rooms of that Empire.

Despite all the upheavals and social changes that have taken place over the last three decades, there still remains an inborn pride and feeling of belonging amongst the majority of Parkhead people. In the words of a popular song, 'If you know your history then you'll know where you're coming from', and I hope that this book will provide some insight into how much Parkhead has contributed, not only to Scots but world history. The motto of William Beardmore, Lord Invernairn, was 'I Commit Myself to Providence', and this is perhaps appropriate as the end of the century approaches. The quotation from Paradise Lost, below, has a particular relevance for Parkhead, with its references to the fiery east (reminiscent of the Forge), not to mention paradise! As the millennium approaches, one can't help but wonder if Paradise Lost might not become Paradise Regained in the hands of future generations.

Charlie McDonald, October 1996.

INTO THE WORLD

They, looking back, all th' eastern side beheld
Of Paradise, so late their happy seat,
Waved over by the flaming brand, the gate
With dreadful faces thronged and fiery arms.
Some natural tears they dropped, but wiped them soon;
The world was all before them, where to choose
Their Place of rest, and Providence their guide
They hand in hand, with wand'ring steps and slow,
Through Eden took their solitary way.

John Milton

Mrs Matilda Porter and her daughter, Mrs Bessie Hogsett, outside their grocers shop in Nisbet Street, 1916.

London Road Co-operative Society was established to meet the everyday needs of the inter-war housing complexes in Dalriada Street, Janefield Street, London Road and Buddon Street. However, with changes in shopping trends and the advent of supermarkets, the Co-op closed in the late 1960s. For a while it was home to an amusement arcade and mini-bingo before becoming a pub in the 1980s. The small newsagents at the far left of the photo was a sweet shop used by countless generations of London Road School pupils, and affectionately known as 'the stalls'.

Flynn's, or the Springfield Vaults, was one of two public houses in Parkhead owned by the well known Glasgow publican Dan Flynn (the other was The Old Straw House). Frequented by parties of mourners drowning their sorrows before and after burials at Dalbeth Cemetery, it was sometime called 'the Funeral Shop'. When the dwellings above the pub were being demolished, local workmen discovered several thousand pounds in old banknotes stashed inside an Oxo cube tin. Fearing that their new-found fortune would be confiscated by the Crown, they sold the banknotes to a local back street businessman for a mere fraction of their value. The Helenvale high rise flats in the background were built by Wimpey between 1967-69 on the site of the Springfield Steel Works. The works were known as 'the pancake' due to the large circular steel plates that were produced there and exported to India for the milling of bread.

Strathclyde Juniors were formed in Dalmarnock in 1893, and later moved to New Springfield Park, Parkhead. The Strathies won the Scottish Junior Cup in 1897, 1907 and 1926, when they beat local rivals Bridgeton Waverley 2-0 after a replay at Firhill. Over 50,000 people attended both games. During the 1931-32 season their goalkeeper Alex Cruickshanks was killed during a game against Rutherglen Glencairn. Both Willie Maley and Bill Struth, managers of Celtic and Rangers respectively, attended his funeral and a memorial to him still stands in the nearby Janefield Cemetery. The Strathies lost the lease of their ground in 1964 and asked the Junior Football Association for permission to play at East Kilbride, a move that was agreed on condition that the club found a ground in Glasgow for the following season. Unable to meet this condition, the Strathies folded, and like Bridgeton Waverley and Parkhead in previous seasons 'died with their boots on'.

The Belvidere Bowling Club Centenary Committee, 1961.
Back row: John Robertson, Wm K. Butler, Peter Taylor, David Hayes, Andrew Roy, Stewart Muir, William Gilmour.
Front row: John Aitken, Robert Donaldson, Robert Loudon, George Wilson, John F. McGhie, Thomas Beveridge.

The Belvidere Bowling Club was formed by a breakaway group from the original Parkhead bowling club, located behind the Bowlers' Rest pub in Tollcross Road. Before settling in Silverdale Street in 1904, the club played on two other greens in Parkhead. Their second location was in Elba Lane, but with the stinking open air middens nearby this was an environmentally unfriendly choice. Silverdale Street, where the club is located now, was originally called Steven Parade, and was named after a local clay brick manufacturer and builder called William Steven.

Macbeth Street, Newbank, photographed in 1930. This is one of several municipal housing schemes that were built in Glasgow during the inter-war years, and along with those in nearby Lilybank, streets in Newbank were named after characters or places in Shakespeare's Macbeth. In February 1936 the Newbank children's playground was opened to the public by councillors and other local dignitaries. According to local newspapers, many of the children were denied use of the large chute and kiddies swings because the officials – still wearing their chains of office – kept queuing up to use them!

West-thorn House was acquired by Thomas Harvie, a Glasgow distiller, in 1819. He built walls on the eastern and western boundaries of his new estate over public footpaths on the banks of the River Clyde, a move that outraged the villagers of Parkhead, Carmyle and Dalmarnock who used the paths. On 21 July 1822, a crowd gathered with crowbars and picks and demolished the offending walls. Shots were fired and the Enniskillen Dragoons were called out, charging into the crowd with sabres drawn before arresting the ringleaders. A protracted court case ensued, brought by local people and funded by public subscriptions and donations. The verdict came out in favour of the people, although Harvie appealed to the House of Lords where he was defeated again. Afterwards, a medal was struck and awarded to several local people 'For successfully defending their right to a path on the banks of the Clyde'. West-thorn House was demolished to make way for the Long John bottling plant.

Parkhead Juniors were founded in 1880, and for many years held the record of having won the Scottish Junior Cup five times. This was a remarkable feat considering that they didn't win the trophy once between 1924 and 1964, when they were forced to disband. Between 1915 and 1926 the Juniors also got to the semi-finals eight times. Their park was originally located on ground between Beattock and Powfoot Streets, but the club later moved to New Helenslea Park in nearby Lilybank. Despite their closeness to Celtic Park they could still draw good home gates even when Celtic were at home, and they attracted a crowd of over 8,000 at one match in 1926. Following several arson attacks on their pavilion in 1964, the club were unable to meet the financial burden of building new facilities. Despite pleas to local businesses for donations, part of Parkhead folklore was allowed to go out of existence for the want of a few hundred pounds in the days before club sponsorship.

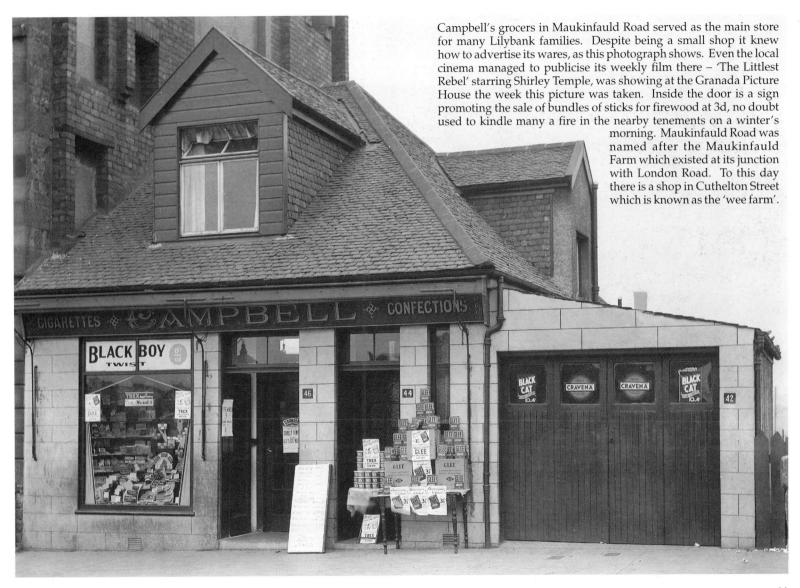

Campbell's grocers in Maukinfauld Road served as the main store for many Lilybank families. Despite being a small shop it knew how to advertise its wares, as this photograph shows. Even the local cinema managed to publicise its weekly film there – 'The Littlest Rebel' starring Shirley Temple, was showing at the Granada Picture House the week this picture was taken. Inside the door is a sign promoting the sale of bundles of sticks for firewood at 3d, no doubt used to kindle many a fire in the nearby tenements on a winter's morning. Maukinfauld Road was named after the Maukinfauld Farm which existed at its junction with London Road. To this day there is a shop in Cuthelton Street which is known as the 'wee farm'.

Quite why Cock Robin and Bobby the Deer have become part of the folklore of Parkhead, Shettleston and Tollcross is hard to explain to anyone born outside the area. Bobby was the last deer to roam free in Tollcross Park, and on his death he was stuffed and put on display in the Tollcross Park Children's Museum, along with the Cock Robin exhibit. The museum closed in 1972, and after years of storage in the basement of Kelvingrove Art Gallery the Cock Robin display was completely renovated for the Glasgow City of Culture Year in 1990. The project was commissioned by the Glasgow East Institute of Social History and Antiquities (GEISHA) and Cock Robin is now loaned to libraries and schools city wide by the Museums Department. The poem 'Who Killed Cock Robin' was written as a satire on Prime Minister Sir Robert Walpole's parliamentary downfall.

Tollcross Mansion dates from 1848 and was built by David Bryce for James Dunlop, whose family founded the Clyde Ironworks. In 1897 the mansion was sold to Glasgow Corporation and opened as a museum in 1905. Due to local government cutbacks it was closed in 1976 and lay derelict until the district council prepared a scheme involving its renovation and conversion into thirteen luxury flats. However, local hostility towards the idea of privatising a community asset resulted in the local authority effectively denying itself planning permission for the scheme. Instead, the house was opened as a sheltered housing complex for the elderly in September 1993 and is run by the Social Work Department in conjunction with the Church of Scotland Social and Responsibility Board. In 1996 the park was allocated money from the National Lottery Fund. This will be spent on a variety of projects, including the restoration of the dilapidated conservatory nearby the Mansion House.

With its view overlooking Tollcross Park, Deerpark Gardens was a desirable residential street, although the herd of deer that it took its name from have long gone. Purchased by Glasgow Corporation for £30,000, Tollcross Park was opened by Lord Provost Richmond on 19 June 1897. Great interest was shown in the event, and an enormous gathering of spectators witnessed the procession of trade union and local friendly societies from Parkhead Cross to the park, led by the silver band from Beardmore's works.

Tollcross Road from the corner of Crail Street. Not much has changed since this photo was taken, except that the tramcars and horse drawn carriages have been replaced with buses and motor cars. Until 1926 this was the junction of Tollcross Road and Great Eastern Road, and many Parkhead folk were of the opinion that the best thing that ever came from Tollcross was the road out of it!

Tollcross Road showing the shops opposite Drumover Drive. Traffic in this picture is sparse compared to the volumes of cars and lorries that use this stretch of road today. In 1920 Parkhead resident Baillie David Willox wrote his memoirs, entitled *The Place, the People and the Pastimes of Parkhead*, for his son Charles who lived in America. At the time there were no houses on the northern side of the road from Sorby Street to Tollcross village, or on most of the land on the south side from Canmore Street, which would still have been part of Maukinfauld Farm then.

Parkhead Model Lodging House was built to accommodate the masses of unskilled labourers who flocked to the area from England and Ireland in search of work in the nineteenth century. When this picture was taken in 1925, the only other building near the lodging house in Quarrybrae Street was Quarrybrae School, which was built between 1902-04. In the last century, a famous industrial dispute took place nearby in Tollcross Road and the Thornhill Path area. Masons and builders of several tenements went on strike because of a cut in wages, and the landlord 'brought in the Irish' as scab labour to complete the building. That stretch of tenements is still referred to as the 'Scabby Loan' by many elderly Parkheadians. The lodging house is currently used as a community centre and college for apprentice gas fitters.

Great Eastern Road and Crail Street, Glasgow

Cochrane's Auld Quarry Knowe Dairy – at the corner of Great Eastern Road and Crail Street – was one of several shops that Cochrane's had in Parkhead. The group of children seem to be showing a keen interest in the steam driven vehicle, whilst in the background the traditional horse drawn wagons are being prepared for their deliveries. In 1926 many street names in Glasgow were renamed to eliminate duplication and Great Eastern Road, which ran from Bellgrove to Drumover Drive, was replaced by the extension of Gallowgate and Tollcross Road.

HRH Duke of York, later King George VI, opened Parkhead Tramway Depot on 2 September 1924. This photograph shows him laying a wreath at the rededication of the Whitevale Depot War Memorial when it was re-sited at Parkhead. The Guard of Honour, proudly wearing their medals, are tramway employees who were veterans of the 15th Glasgow Tramways Battalion of the Highland Light Infantry. Thousands of men were recruited from the Glasgow tram depots by the bearded James Dalrymple, manager of the Tramways Department, on the left of this picture. So many of their workforce had enlisted by 1915 that Glasgow became the first city in Britain to use women tram conductors, which it did for the duration of the war. The Duke drove a tramcar from the depot along Great Eastern Road, later opening Helenvale Park and watching the first match to be played there (a 6-1 win for Rangers against Partick Thistle).

The Tollcross Tavern, photographed before it was revamped in 'Tudorbethan' style in 1930. A local veto poll was held in Parkhead in 1921, and the majority of mainly female voters elected to abolish all pubs in the area, making Parkhead dry. This shock result was cancelled the next day when it became clear that the polling booths had been opened so late in the morning that the working men had been unable to register their vote. So Parkhead went to the polls again, and decided to keep the pubs open during normal licence hours.

Taken in 1961, this back court picture shows the type of building that would have stood in Parkhead prior to its redevelopment at the turn of the century. This block stood in Tollcross Road, between Burgher Street and Helenvale Street, and was demolished in 1980. Over the years it housed a variety of shops including a jewellers, cobblers, chiropodists, and hairdressers, with a school of motoring upstairs. This was probably the property that David Willox described in his memoirs as having weaving shops on the ground floor, with dwellings upstairs.

This block, once home to a pawnbroker's, was being advertised by Grant & Wilson (who still trade from Bridgeton Cross today) as up for sale in 1939. No doubt it came as a pleasant surprise to the people of Parkhead when the building was bought by the F.W. Woolworth chain. They provided a service in Parkhead for over four decades, before the shop became a victim of their empire sell-off. Thousands of Parkhead children would have had their Fair Fortnight clothes and plastic sandals bought from these premises, not to mention the plastic Beatles wigs that Woolworth's sold for half a crown in the swinging sixties!

Parkhead Cross, probably photographed from the former Glasgow Corporation Transport Tower at the junction of Westmuir Street and Tollcross Road. The name Parkhead comes naturally enough from its position at 'the head of the park', and the lands that made up the park were previously part of the Belvidere estate (now attached to Belvidere hospital). The name Parkhead cannot be traced any further back than the Statistical Account of 1791, although at that time the inns there were used as a stopping place for the London mail coaches.

Parkhead Cross, traditionally known as 'the Sheddens', lost its rural setting with the rapid expansion of Beardmore's Parkhead Works and the need for additional housing to accommodate the massive influx of workers. The Watson family, who owned the local grocers, were responsible for building many of the tenements around the Cross. Legend has it that they were set a friendly challenge by a rival builder to see who could build the finer tenement, and the Watsons were judged winners on account of having carved the heads of the family in prominent positions on their building. The tenement is situated at the corner of Duke Street and Westmuir Street, and replaced the white building in this picture. The Watson Fund, which is still in existence, was bequeathed by the family for the benefit of Parkhead widows and orphans, although it stipulates that only Presbyterians can apply.

SPRINGFIELD ROAD, PARKHEAD, GLASGOW.

A.4955.

The top end of Springfield Road in the 1960s. The stretch of road from Parkhead Cross to London Road was once known as Dalmarnock Street. Previous to this it was called Dry Thrapple Loan because of the clouds of stour which blew up from it before it was metalled. Cook's Bookshop once supplied reading material for generations of Parkhead folk, providing a weekly source of Commando comics for budding Action Man role-models of the 1960s. Dansken and Fletcher, factors of several Parkhead properties, had their office here, before they became Hacking & Paterson the Estate Agents.

Beardmore's and many other heavy industrial works in Parkhead were turned over to making munitions during the Second World War, thereby making them potential targets for the Luftwaffe. In fact, many local folk claim that William Joyce – 'Lord Haw-Haw', the Nazi propagandist – frequently referred to Parkhead Forge as the 'toy shop' in his nightly 'Germany Calling' radio broadcasts. This group of Parkhead evacuees muster at Newlands School with their nametags, tin mugs, and cardboard boxes containing gas masks, before heading for the station in nearby Whitby Street. The vast majority of local children were evacuated to villages and towns in Dumfriesshire.

Miss Duff's class, Newlands School, 1930. The school was built in 1896 and – on the proviso that it always be used for community and educational purposes – the land was gifted to the school board of the time by Lord Newlands. In the 1970s Strathclyde Regional Council closed the school. Their intention was to sell the property for use as small industrial units, but they were prevented when the campaigning Parents' Action Group found records detailing the original gift in the Hozier Family papers. Until 1994 the building was used as the headquarters of the South East District Social Work Department before it was closed for renovation. Its future is currently uncertain as it is considered to be surplus to requirement by the new District Council.

The last row of traditional hand loom weavers' cottages in Parkhead stood in Springfield Road, and was used as a newsagent's with an attached residence until it was destroyed by fire about 1980. In 1817 the weavers of Parkhead and Camlachie formed their own quasi-Masonic brotherhood to protect their rights to maintain the price of the cloth that they manufactured. The original address of the Radical Risings of 1820 was also drawn up at a meeting held in one of these cottages in 1819. By 1837, during another period of recession, a new working class reform movement – Chartism – had emerged, and the weavers of Parkhead were committed to the six points of the People's Charter. An opening beside the cottage led to 'backlands' which consisted of two storey cottage-type housing. These houses, with an outside stair giving access to the top flat, were once described as 'groups of lightless, unventilated clotted masses of slum' and posed a constant problem for sanitary and public health officials.

The Glasgow Eastern Automobile Company's garage in Dalmarnock Street (Springfield Road), photographed in 1923. The two boys were perhaps waiting to 'catch a niggy' on the back of a works van or lorry. The garage later belonged to J.R. Adams the scrap merchant, who had long connections with the district until recently. J. Kane Fireplaces now occupy the premises.

The W.A. Smith Hardware Emporium on the corner of Edmiston Drive and Dalmarnock Street (Springfield Road), later Ward's, supplied every household necessity in the 1920s. It was possible to be born in Springfield Road, be educated in Newlands School, spend a lifetime working in Springfield Steel Foundry, get married, furnish a home, raise a family, pass your leisure time in the local pubs and the Black Cat Cinema, retire, return to Newlands Day Centre as a patient, die and be laid to rest in the Eastern Necropolis (Janefield Cemetery), without ever having to move any more than quarter of a mile from your home. Such was the social and commercial structure of the area from the 1920s to the late 1970s that this 'cradle to grave' scenario was actually the life story of one of the elderly people who attended Newlands Day Centre in the 1980s.

The Sharpe Memorial Church of the Nazarene was named after George Sharpe, who left Parkhead Congregational Church in 1906 to found the first Holiness Pentecostal Church in Scotland. Over the years, Parkhead has had an abundance of churches, with at least three in Burgher Street alone at one time. Due to falling congregations in the 1960s, many churches were forced to amalgamate. The present Calton Parkhead Church in Helenvale Street, which was opened in 1935, now houses the combined congregations of Parkhead East and West Churches.

This building in Burgher Street was demolished in 1960 and may well have been the one that David Willox mentions in his memoirs 'as rather pretentious for those days, consisting of one block with two dwelling houses of room, and kitchen and mid-room and a four loom and six loom shop beneath'. The family had strong connections with Burgher Street.

Parkhead Railway Station was renamed Parkhead Stadium in 1952, because of its proximity to Celtic's ground. This picture was taken in June 1963, before the station became a victim of Dr Beeching's axing of the railway network. Celtic Park's floodlights were first switched on on 12 October 1959 for a friendly against the then English champions, Wolverhampton Wanderers, who won 2-0. At 208 feet above the playing surface, the floodlights were believed to be the highest in the world. In July 1914 King George V, Queen Mary and their entourage disembarked here for the royal visit to Beardmore's Parkhead Works. Whitby Street, which overlooked the station, was called Winston Street at the time in honour of Winston Churchill, who had married Clementine Hozier, a niece of Lord Newlands. In 1989 the derelict railway station was filled in and landscaped.

The General Wolfe pub stood on the corner of Gallowgate and Millerston Street before being demolished in 1986. It took its name from General James Wolfe, the 'Saviour of Quebec', who scaled the Heights of Abraham and won Canada for the British in 1759, although he was killed in his hour of glory. As Lieut Colonel of Sackville's Regiment during 1749 and 1750, Wolfe and his men were billeted with the people of Glasgow as there was no barracks in the city. Wolfe resided in Camlachie Mansion, and was remembered by the villagers for his tall and slender appearance, riding to and from Camlachie on a spirited grey charger. In a letter to a fellow officer, dated 2 April 1749, he wrote 'the women here [in Glasgow], are coarse, cold and cunning, for ever enquiring after men's circumstances. They make that the standard of good breeding. You may well imagine it would not be difficult for me to be pretty well received here if I took pains, having some of the advantages necessary to recommend me to their favour.' Camlachie mansion was later converted into shops and a public house before being demolished in 1932.

Camlachie Mansion was built in 1720 by Sir James Walkinshaw of Barrowfield, the prominent Jacobite. He was taken prisoner during the Battle of Sheriffmuir, and later escaped from Stirling Castle by exchanging clothes with his wife. Shortly afterwards, Walkinshaw's tenth daughter was born, and Princess Clementina Sobieski, mother of Charles Edward Stuart, stood as her godmother and gave her her own name, Clementina. On his retreat from Derby in 1745, Bonnie Prince Charlie visited Glasgow and met the young Clementina Walkinshaw. She later became his mistress and bore him a daughter named Charlotte. The relationship was a stormy one. Charles became jealous of Clementina's charms and surrounded their bed with bells which would ring if anyone came near. However, this was one bed that she had made and was not prepared to lie in, and she ran off with one of her admirers, taking her daughter with her. The old mansion is best remembered as Wolfe's house.

Despite their name, Bridgeton Waverley were very much a Parkhead club, and their original ground was in Camlachie prior to the building of Barrowfield Housing Scheme. Their new ground, New Barrowfield on London Road, is now the Celtic training ground. The club won the Scottish Juvenile Cup in the first three years of its inception, turned junior in 1924, and came runners-up in the Scottish Junior Cup Finals of 1926 and 1934. Many of their players went professional, the most notable being Tommy Law of Chelsea and Scotland, one of the legendary Wembley Wizards of 1928. Ex-Waverley player and Parkhead born Joe O'Neill scored four goals for Aberdeen when they beat Rangers 6-1 in the 1954 League Cup Semi-Final. Having played their last games at Carntyne Dog Track, the club went defunct in 1962. However, they were reformed in 1976 by the author, and their name lives on in the Scottish Amateur Football League.

From 1870, Vinegarhill showground was the main open air entertainment ground in Glasgow. In 1891 Buffalo Bill Cody came to the East End Exhibition in Dennistoun with his 'Wild West Show', a circus with cowboys, rodeo riders and real Red Indian braves. The Indians camped in Vinegarhill during their stay, and according to local lore Cody and his entourage frequented the Coffin Bar in nearby Whitevale Street – no doubt for their two fingers of red-eye. Some of the Native Americans didn't move on with the show, and their relatives are still living in and around Glasgow. Vinegarhill was acquired by the Green family prior to the First World War, during which they erected a gigantic wooden effigy of the Kaiser, which people hammered nails into in return for making a donation to the War Effort Fund. The Greens later became famous Glasgow cinema magnates, most famously owning the 4,400 seater Playhouse in Renfield Street, better known in modern times as The Apollo.

Camlachie Jail, which stood until 1977, was located at the junction of Yate Street and Gallowgate. Over the years it was used for a variety of different purposes, including serving as a lamplighter's office. The tower contained dwellings for several families and the four clocks were called 'the four faced liars' because none of them ever told the same time. The famous Camlachie Institute, renowned for its political debates, stood across the street. Many famous politicians spoke there including Cunningham-Graham and Keir Hardie. An interesting landmark, consisting of cobbles shaped in the form of a ball, boot, leg and goal posts, can still be seen outside the site of the jail in Yate Street. Many have tried to link it to the Celtic and Scotland goalkeeper John Thomson, who was so tragically killed whilst playing against Rangers at Ibrox in September 1931, but the story of the stones goes back further than that. The landmark was constructed by a local workman named O'Malley who was carrying out some repairs to the cobble stones and was being pestered by children. In order to carry on with his work he set the children the task of finding odd shaped stones which he shaped into this design. Camlachie, which means 'the muddy bend on the burn' was famous for her cooperages. At one time there were nine, the last of these closing their doors in 1990.

Founded in 1760, the Black Bull claims to be the oldest pub in Parkhead. It was once noted for its regular penny reels, a sort of eighteenth century disco whereby the men would pay a penny for the privilege of dancing with a woman – or as Willox refers to the female sex, 'a pick-up'. The Black Bull was also immortalised in a poem by the Parkhead poet, John Breckenbridge. The out-buildings and brewing houses of Andrew Stout, a one-time landlord, stood behind the pub. He manufactured lemonade, ginger beer and soda water on the premises, and was eventually bought out by A.G. Barr, a company which grew from humble beginnings to become one of the world's top producers of soft drinks.

A regular event for most public houses in the east end in the forties and fifties was the annual bus run, when the punters would set off for their chosen destination, loaded up with the obligatory cases of screwtops and an accordion. This Old Straw House outing was heading for Burntisland in 1949. The pub's name comes from the time when Lanarkshire farmers used to bring their straw into Parkhead village and leave it around the inn, where it was picked up by the Glasgow stableowners. At one stage there were at least sixty-six public houses in the Gallowgate from Parkhead Cross to Glasgow Cross.

The King's Cafe in the Gallowgate was one of many ice-cream parlours and fish restaurants set up by Italian immigrants in Parkhead. At one time these cafes were considered to be dens of iniquity. Young people reputedly spent too much time loafing around there, while the newly established cafe owners aggravated the Established Church by opening their doors on a Sunday and breaking the traditional Sabbath. At the turn of the century, there were also claims that ice-cream could spread bacteria. But despite all these tribulations, the Italian-style fast food shops and cafes prospered in Parkhead, although the eating habits of some Glaswegians have changed from Scottish-Italian fare to Asian cuisine in recent years.

W.&J. Bowie offered a top-class laundry service to the populace of Parkhead from their premises at 1420 Gallowgate, directly opposite the Old Straw House. Lloyd's the Fishmonger's, one of the many fresh fish and poultry outlets in and around Parkhead Cross, stood next door and now trades as Taggart's Fish and Chicken Bar.

The City Bakeries' tea rooms at Parkhead Cross provided tea and buns for many thousands of customers over the years. A large seating area at the back was used as a regular eating and meeting place by businessmen and locals alike. Next door was Maypole's the Grocers, famous for its Empire Butter and other brand-name products when this picture was taken in the 1930s. The doorway behind the woman and child was the entrance to Dansken's Stationery Shop. This was run for many years by a spinster daughter of Dansken the Factor. The family never recovered from the loss of their son James Angus Dansken who died of his wounds in a German Prisoner of War Camp during the First World War. It was during this war that bakers such as the City Bakeries renamed the traditional German biscuit the Empire Biscuit to show their patriotism. The tea rooms closed in the 1980s and the site is now home to offices of the East End Information Project.

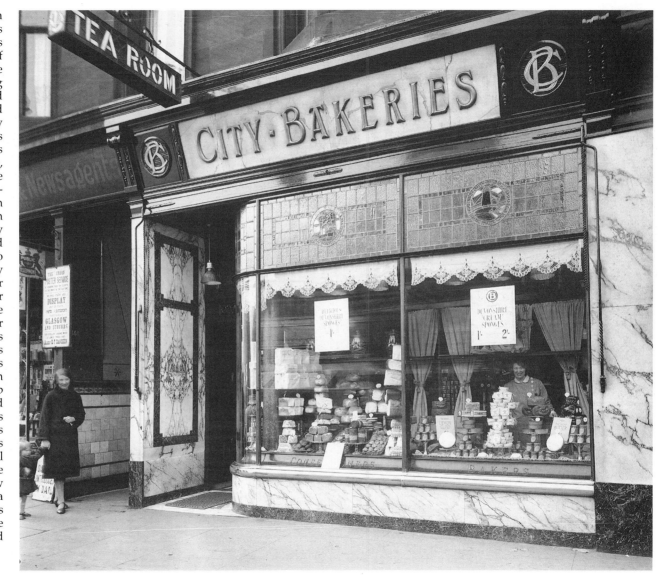

The regular crossing of Duke Street by railway engines travelling from one side of Beardmore's Works to the other was a familiar scene in Parkhead. There were two sets of gates at these level crossings, one known as the white gates, and many a person was made late for work or an appointment when their transport was unfortunate enough to be stopped at these crossings. After the Great War, William Beardmore was dubbed 'The Field Marshall of Industry' because of his contribution to the manufacture of weapons.

The Royal Visit of King George V and Queen Mary in July 1914 was one of the most spectacular occasions ever witnessed in Parkhead. The Royal couple's cortege left the prettily decorated Parkhead Station for Parkhead Forge, led by the Scots Greys through streets lined with thousands of spectators. This Royal Arch in Duke Street was built by the workers of Beardmore's. Many were veterans of the Boer War and acted as a Guard of Honour during the visit, being presented with a specially struck medal to mark the event afterwards. After inspecting the works, Queen Mary was presented with a magnificent bouquet by Annie Dunlop of Parkhead Primary, who was lowered down in a crane to make the presentation. Within a month of the visit, Britain had declared war on Germany and Beardmore's became one of the country's main weapons manufacturers. Several strikes were held during the war years, and these were immediately cracked down upon by the Government, with several of the ringleaders being exiled to Edinburgh!

St Michael's Primary School and Roman Catholic Church in Nisbet Street, (photographed in 1960), acted as an educational and spiritual facility for Parkhead Catholics. The needs of some poorer parishioners were instrumental in the formation of Celtic Football Club in 1887, one of the aims of which was to provide funds for food kitchens in the Missions of St Michael's and other Roman Catholic parishes. The chapel, established c.1876, moved to the present St Michael's Church in the Gallowgate in May 1970. Although the new church has no tower, there is a tall tapered brick pier surmounted by a figure of St Michael the Archangel. During the First World War nearly 500 Parkhead men paid 'the ultimate sacrifice', and it is therefore fitting that in the absence of a Parkhead War Memorial, a magnificent oak figure of St Michael hangs from the vaulted roof of the Scottish National War Memorial in Edinburgh Castle. The casket containing the Roll of Honour with the names of the 100,000 Scots who died in The Great War lies beneath the figure.

The girls of St Michael's Primary at play during their morning break. Shortly after this photograph was taken in 1961 the school moved to the new purpose built site in Springfield Road.

The original Parkhead Post Office was located at the Sheddens at Parkhead Cross, and was run by Gibbie Watson, the postmaster and baker of the village. Later, the post office moved to Duke Street (above), before moving to Springfield Road in the sixties. The Duke Street building then became a restaurant belonging to the Amato family, initally called La Bon Appetit and later becoming the Duke of Torraine. Afterwards, it was a bar/diner called Antlers (later Hiccups).

WESTMUIR STREET, PARKHEAD, GLASGOW.   A.4953.

Westmuir Street, looking east towards Parkhead Cross. This was the original thoroughfare through the hamlet of Westmuir. Traditionally a mining village, the colliers would eke out an existence from nearby pits such as the Caroline and Westmuir. In 1679 a party of Covenanters took refuge here after a skirmish with John Graham of Claverhouse and his troops at Glasgow Cross. The Parkhead and Westmuir Economic Society was one of the first co-operative groups in the world, and was started by the weavers and the miners of Parkhead village.

Parkhead Public School, which closed in 1963, was the oldest school in the area. During the First World War many Belgian refugees settled in the east end, and some of their children attended Parkhead Primary. This postcard was sent by one of these children, and the message on the back is written in French. An extract from the school log book of the time states that 'In view of possible air-raids by the enemy, a scheme has been worked out whereby all the classes on the second and third floors will march down to the ground floor in each building. Arrangements in regard to water buckets and phone service have also been made.' These precautions were introduced after German Zeppelin attacks on the east coast of Britain. The Grassmarket in Edinburgh was hit by air-raids, as were the North Yorkshire towns of Scarborough and Whitby. Wintson Street was later renamed Whitby Street in remembrance of one of these attacks.

The children of Miss Yuill's infant class, Parkhead Primary School, 1922. The school kept excellent log books detailing its day to day running, and had the distinction of receiving regular visits from William Beardmore at the annual prize-giving ceremonies. When it closed for the summer holidays in June 1914, Parkhead Primary's headmaster gave a picture show to celebrate the 600th anniversary of the battle of Bannockburn. After the show patriotic songs were sung and the children were dispersed for the school holidays. They were not to know that within weeks many of their families would have to apply to the School Board for free books as their fathers became involved in another patriotic war; supposedly 'the war to end all war'.

The Fyfe and Douglas Coffin Works factory was based in Nisbet Street and Salamanca Street and built for Chichton and Moore around 1896 as the Phoenix Cabinet Works. They supplied coffins for Funeral Directors all over the world until their closure in the late 1970s. Parkhead White Rose, a juvenile football side, were said to have worn jerseys, embroidered with silk roses, and made from linen used to line the coffins